LOST DIARY

Pages

FREEDOM IN A BUSY MIND:
POETRY & PROSE

JESSICA FULLER

Lost Diary Pages

Freedom in a Busy Mind

Poetry & Prose

**Selections written by
Jessica Fuller**

Jessica Fuller
https://jusjesspoetry.org
Grace 4 Purpose, Publishing Co LLC
contact@grace4purposeco.com
ISBN: 979-8-9926893-7-2
Printed in the United States of America

Dedicated to the past versions of myself, each a placeholder with a unique purpose, now laid to rest as I appreciate each present moment that comes my way.

When you scribble your secrets down on paper, it's like watching the geese flying scenes in Fly Away Home. Amy did a big thing and was so brave. When I see geese flying in their migrating pattern, I often envy them. What does it feel like to fly?

This book is not just a book that playfully mentions traumatic experiences in comical or questionable ways. This book is a spicy dance around deep topics and experiences. It is a tango between truth and avoidance, denial and fear, rage and acceptance, masculine and feminine. This book is about the freedom found in one mind among billions in this multifaceted human experience.

Lost Diary Pages

Not to be read in any specific order.

The Stories We Tell Our Children

Could it be that "misfit" was never a thing to bear shame

For even I burrowed deep

To connect identity to a name

And maybe my babies do smile in their sleep

As mother's brush with a flame

Led to a series of reap-ing

Identifying

Still trying

No denying

Truth?

PERMISSION

Give yourself permission to put yourself first.
Never allow anyone or anything
to make you question your worth.
You have purpose on this earth.

I write to and for those who are fighting. Still fighting.

Sometimes we chase what isn't meant for us,
acceptance causing us to excavate
those comfortably hidden qualities
that we need to address
in order to step into our greatest
and best versions of ourselves,
who we were always destined to be.

Give yourself permission to strive for success,
Knowing that success looks different to us all.

Encapsulated: Fury of the Pen

Quite odd,
high levels of vulnerability?
Masking
to bask in a likeness won't quite cut it for this part,
not for me.

The way she walks and how she talks
you can tell that she's been through a storm.

The way she gravitates and radiates,
you can feel it - what she speaks is real.

Glittery glimmers far better than disdain,
that encapsulated dream she will always remain.

Yes, this is what a journey is made of.

******

I write like I am mad, many days I am mad, but more
often than not I cannot figure out what I am mad
about. Not mad but perhaps I've had enough of
halfway manifesting, not blind but tiptoeing around
whilst inside a feverous calling towards more ignites a
fury in my pens and on my keyboards.

Breathing

The ease of written words expelled.
The release of a busy mind.
Much like breathing.

There is a path before me, and I wonder who else can
see it,
Intrinsically pulled
Ought I quiet these paced steps as I ponder?

There is a path before me and I no longer care what it
looks like from the outside.
I am bruised, worn, and often probably tired
But I won't stop walking.

When society says, "slow down"
I beg of it pardon
and ask it politely not to project such standards onto
me.
I'm okay nowadays, learning ways to cope, learning
how to pamper my neurodiversity.
When someone asks me why I do so much research
I simply think of Mama and how much everything
makes sense now.

Adversity to Determination

I'm going somewhere, and I won't be there tomorrow
but patience and determination serve me well
nowadays.

Maya Angelou speaks of stimulated nervous systems
and upset digestive tracts,

I want to look back and say,

"I wouldn't take nothing back," too.

I've been feeling a way, but she also says that oppressors
are children of God,

and so are those who I think I forgave

and am still forgiving,

myself included.

This poem quotes Maya Angelou's, "Wouldn't Take Nothing for My Journey Now."

Angelou, Maya. Wouldn't Take Nothing for My Journey Now. Narrated by Maya Angelou. Random House Audio, 2005. **https://www.audible.com/pd/Wouldnt-Take-Nothing-for-My-Journey-Now-Audiobook/B002VACQ0O**

FAST LANE

I remember this girl of a woman

Who'd leave everything behind

Leaving trails of unfinished business

And unanswered questions

To hop

From state to state

Coast to coast

Instead of seeing a hard thing through.

When I

Stare in the mirror long enough,

She looks like someone I used to know

Or be.

Someone who threw in the towel

And laced up her shoes

Took a drive

Hopped a plane

Took the fast lane

All the way to nowhere

Just to start over again.

Dodgeball

Accounta- what?   Shut up.

    Acceptance -

Grips chest   Acknowledges.   Falls.

Owns.   Wait a second.

        Transfer.   Back peddles.

  Reckless - wreck this.

Excuse.   Fast. Fear. Fall.
Fight. Flight.   Gets it right.

      Swimming   Fun   Ego   Bliss

Pride   Hypocrisy   Hit or miss.

Bandage.
Transfer - Energy.

Music.   Dances. Escapes. Over-compensates.

Insecure.   Self-righteous. Human.

CONSCIOUS MUSIC

I write to be free yet I write to be me yet I write
sparingly lately.
I blend in.

Not blaming my past but the past has had a grasp on
me these last
few years. Yet, ahead I see -

fast life half wife dim light
still, fight.

Flirting with the moon,
electrically swoon,
and in a room I am but an ambient reflection.

Scrape off the burnt parts

Shake a leg can't afford to beg

was it sugar and spice, or

am I always too nice?

The batter made a splatter

and interpersonal becomes too flaky

too dense, but it's baking

crumbly cookies and buttery bread

devil's food cake to equate to decadence

but I love chocolate on chocolate.

Richness can't be bought or explained.

I like a sprinkle of onion and garlic powder

and yes on some days

I make it with love and on other days with

too much trauma,

watered down succulence

as I keep praying for Mama.

Fourteen

The inappropriate use of humor is often used as a coping strategy. Or a defense mechanism. Or maybe both.

The adults were right, I wasn't ready. $500.

101 days, 101 ways to self-inflict pain.

Tiny human on screen seen in between gasps of gas.

My young heart also mangled into pieces.

But a little counseling after the fact wouldn't have killed me, either.

******

Alice Walker speaks of when not to give your body to others: when drunk, when you feel sorry for someone, out of contempt, out of curiosity, out of only passion. At a tender age, I went through something similar to Alice, and while she kept hers a secret from her mother for about a decade, my experience left me riddled with guilt, regret, and many odd feelings. For years.

******

For years I exclaimed, "I don't want a husband," because for years my world consisted of choosing a side. You are either straight or you are gay. You are lesbian or you're bisexual. If you're bisexual, the lesbians don't want you, and if you say that you're a lesbian, the egos of many men become aggrieved. You then risk arming them with an additional chip or reason to seek validation. If identifying as pansexual, people may have to run a Google search before they shape their judgments of you.

To not want a husband, or a wife, is not such a despairing thing. I find that I have given love, or several false concepts of love, enough attempts to warrant closing the book of naive and lustful dreams until I am more firm in my career, my destiny, and in me.

This piece references a personal experience shared by Alice Walker in "Gathering Blossoms Under Fire."

Boyd, Valerie and Walker, Alice. Gathering Blossoms Under Fire - The Journals of Alice Walker. Narrated by Aunjanue Ellis, Alice Walker, and Janina Edwards.Simon & Schuster Audio, 2022. https://www.audible.com/pd/Gathering-Blossoms-Under-Fire-Audiobook/1797118625.

Train of Dreams, Fragments of Self

In a valley of dreams

Subconscious desires

And brushes with fantasy intertwine

With imprints of a tainted past, a

Series of events longing to be washed away, wiped clean

So that my working memory may work more
effectively. In the valley of my dreams

I feel the pain of my enemies

But during my waking hours I need not

Enable my empathy

To become recurring nightmares

That I have freed myself from.

In the valley of my hidden dreams,

I am what I once was,

Hence my sympathy.

No one's home

Vulnerability doesn't live here. There's no space for it, and if there are crumbs of it laying around, the roaches probably got to them. I want to share my worries but when I step inside of perfection, they disappear. Immaculate homes and high status. There are no worries here. It's like a skin picking, lip shaking fight to control my mouth and impulses. When I grow up, I'll be the best at everything. My house will stay clean just in case someone comes over without calling first.

I want -

I want to ~~be happy~~.

I want to ~~be free~~.

I want to be liked.

I want to be like them.

I want ~~stability~~.

I need money.

I want to have nice cars and money hidden in my socks.

~~I want to have it all.~~

I need ~~that them him her~~ me.

VHS

Rewind.

Perfection, I was told, doesn't exist. But I have been looking for it in other people. I have been expecting it from myself, all the while praying to God in gratitude, forgetting that no matter what list of plans I prepare and present, God has the final say. Uncertainty makes me feel "crazy," more crazy than acquiring degrees and accolades to prove to anyone that I am worthy. I become discombobulated when met with uncertainty, and for a while it seems that all of my tools and strategies are further in the distance, no longer within an arm's length of my grasp.

Fast forward.

And so, when things change, I notice. I really, really notice. A shift in the atmosphere, a change in a person's mannerisms, when someone is having a bad day. A walk that is a different walk, a limp today that wasn't there yesterday. A message. A thread of messages. A facial tic. A clear of the throat, the sound of keys versus the sound of a belt coming your way. Conversations, how voices elevate but not too much. No need to worry tonight. Sleep may become me.

Press play.

People say that I am strong. What exactly do they mean? People also call me crazy, so there you go.

17

Bittersweet, Me.

To see with clarity is first bittersweet,

sifting through shards

seeking to piece me

back together.

But then -

I remember when I lived on that street, the beat box of struggle

and jump rope.

I don't expect wholeness

each time that I reflect on a

mess that I've made. Wading in

my sorrows keeps me stuck.

Now I cope to broaden the scope of my imaginative, creative, and spiritual thoughts.

I can't turn down that road where dreams and dead animals rot.

I snuck in a lot

of little creatures on Academy Street,

wild rabbits and frogs

and kittens and dogs -

but I couldn't sustain them

in modes of secrecy.

They completed me

much like this craft of

writing,

much like true love

that is poetry.

You can't find yourself while hiding within others.

Identity consists of many things and

individuality is negated through shape shifting.

Sticky Thoughts

Pushing herself through layers of comfortable patterns
in the face of adversity,

She took off her running shoes.

There was a hole in one sole, anyway.

She smelled like coconut oil and lavender,

Freshly fallen from a cliff that left her descending too far
into her thoughts.

Fall was always transformative for her,

But those sticky thoughts rooted in fear longed to lead
her to a mindset of defeat.

She refused. She was tired, the remnants of zip codes
and time zones

Spun into a delicate web of

"I've come too far."

Instead, she'd do that thing that she always loved,

And she'd live to breathe calmly another night.

THEY BURN THEIR BRAS, DON'T THEY?

If I stand in front of society bleeding these lines of
poetry,
I ought not be too radical.
Who knew that during the most historical feminist
movements,
Leaders didn't actually burn their bras?

I never felt more like a lost feather gracefully landing
here or there, or
Why glimpses of romanticism felt like, "I belong there,"
Or why pages of transcendental voices sounded like
someone I used to know.

I told you all that this poetry writing thing,

It's a lifestyle that I am destined for.

Spreading the awareness of this human existence,

Some days it comes out like shit.

But on some days, it comes out nicely wrapped,

In a beautiful form,

And either way I bleed it. I need it.

Emotion is most of what I know,

Not so much the regulating of it but

I feel so intensely, immensely driven by the weight of
every single one.

Yes, I must fine tune my mindfulness

As a gift won't go far rooted in rage.

My soul is set ablaze each time that I

Read feel breathe in

The depths of greatness.

If I could sit down with Alice Walker or Evie Shockley,

To have crossed paths with Maya Angelou or Audre
Lorde…

If I stand in front of society bleeding these lines of poetry,

I won't be too radical.

Even during the most historical feminist movements,

Leaders didn't actually burn their bras.

Yet had I been there, surely I would have been the one to take it too far,

Waving my burning bra and loose bits everywhere,

Completely messing up the message.

I've got a message or two,

But they won't get through if I keep stepping on my toes

With these damn arthritic feet,

These neurodivergent qualities.

NO NAME

lost diary pages

disintegrate into the distance of

a fast paced lifestyle

survival mode of our loved ones

understood but unacknowledged

as a contributing factor to a rapture

of a different kind.

THIRTEEN

I do wish I'd known that

I wasn't in the wrong,

being 13 and him being in his 30's.

Autumn leaves, railroad tracks.

Yale Avenue.

Regurgitate

I talk a little too much a little too often.
I love the idea of the gift of introspection, but my
goodness, it's hard for me to just say or think nothing.

How often do you say something that you think about
later, for hours?

AMELIORATE

Don't tell me to go at your pace,

I stalled for years before getting back into this race and

Who knew that a race need not be a race at all,

Standing on my own two feet though I'm not very tall

Tall tales and good wishes, fragments of broken dishes
and projected expectations.

I expect a lot from myself - and am deserving of such.

I stumbled upon a place called "Girl, you are worthy,"

longing only for alleviation from self-love and
persistence's touch

and now I see that my existence matters.

Floating Hope

We float on hopes and prayers,

too stubborn to sink,

arms strong but aching.

Unconventional Woman, Love Yourself

It is becoming increasingly difficult to downplay my dreams,
And so I no longer will.
I tell myself that it's okay to have just realized a thing or two.

I show myself grace as I trace
These fine lines on my body
With my fingertips.

What is a life without a journey well narrated?

Foolish accounts of foolish nights
Wearing admirable uniforms
Feeling like somebody,
When really I was just a naive teen
Running away from her hometown and her past.

What I found
Was something similar
To that warmth in the pit of my stomach
When I open a book written by an unconventional woman,

The kind who isn't so agreeable.

Something like pride or purpose.

When did you first start feeling like someone?

It is true that whatever I do, I put my whole self into it.
Some say this is foolish, and while I now know that
mindfulness is key,
I told you that I cannot do "surface level" or "bare
minimum."

Solitude brought to me
A closer connection to God
And a stronger desire to succeed.

I never in my life *wanted* to settle,
Always that temperamental oddball who really didn't fit
in *anywhere*.

It is becoming increasingly difficult to downplay my
dreams,
And so I no longer will.

Fear tried to hold me and keep me feeling incapable yet
I have surpassed my own goals when it comes to

fulfilling roles that keep my soul aflame and continue to heal my inner child.

Oh, Calm Down.

Step left step right

Step inside of the square,

Tap left shoulder then tap the right,

Step on crack break Mama's back

*Better step with this foot to undo the step made
with that foot*

Don't split the pole? Which way is splitting it?

Ladders, black cats, red birds, dirty bedroom.

He mad.

Mama sad.

Juneteenth Poetry

I breathe in a right that I've often taken for granted, for ancestral backs may have turned when I longed not to exist,

twisting and testing fate,

chained to my woes and excuses

and valid traumatic experiences.

I appreciate a journey that I couldn't predict, longing to find my place,

my identity, which parts of culture defined me, and which parts shunned me.

Resolutions I sought,

approaches a bit extreme I'll admit,

wanting to know that I, too am heard and seen yet I cannot and will not forget

the foundational strides of loved ones gone

as I stand for my own equality driven causes, lest I be the hypocrite that I've been afraid to become my whole life.

Words that whistle in the wind

***Fear statement: I just want to tell my own story
before I am unable to.***

I think there's a saying

About how we don't know what life will bring

Or that we cannot predict the

Things that come along to challenge

Our will or that sometimes

Things happen that leave us speechless

Or leave us carrying a few ounces

Of regret, bellies full of force-fed wisdom or

Strength that we find when we least expect it or a

Love that outweighs pounds of unanswered questions
inside the heart of a teenage girl.

None of those things matter now.

But if we can grieve past versions of ourselves

Or those we lay to rest

Or sprinkle into the sea,

Can we too grieve a memory

Or several as they flee from the mind of someone else?

There I go thinking outside the mind,

Cognition is a gift that can't defeat the toils of ticking time.

And no, I don't want to talk about it.

This Part

There's a steady drip dropping

        From the faucet,

I'm so grateful to have this second bathroom,

Airplanes taking off in the not so distant sky but my oh my I pay the rent on my own in this three bedroom apartment home,

Pretty fancy these thin walls are.

        I hear everything!

    There's a steady beat pounding in my heart and in my soul,

Destiny calls to me, and fate is so hard to control

Much like a stream of thoughts

That I had no other choice but to jot down.

Back to sleep, Poet.

But I am awake, wanting to pour pounds of love and good cooking onto my kids' plates each and everyday, not

Just for a couple weeks after payday.

Struggle is a mindset that need not be a norm but how normal is it to constantly be stressed? Now I'm taking strides as deep breaths exude my chest.

I think I'm ready for this part.

Honey Suckles

I always ran away from bees

yet I long to run through

a field of flowers as my eleven year old self,

catching rays of sunlight that illuminate

reddish brown arm hairs, natural musk

permeating the air because I beat the boys

in football, sharp blades of grass standing

higher than the weeds -

We found honeysuckles.

<u>Prosperity Pathway</u>

An image I stumbled upon

Entranced I was because

The closer

I stepped to it the

More clear she became

The more connected

I've ever felt to a name

And now

Each decade of trials

They

Seem to make

Sense.

I do not desire decadence

I only desire for me to make sense

And since making a series

Of choices I see -

I feel

An integration of sorts,

No longer

Are my visions full of distorted

Confused

And

Blurred disarray.

Yes, this path is often lonely

But on this path I choose

To stay.

Prosperity.

Fairytale Fantasy

Imprints of a mirror once propped upon the wall,
I know that I'll catch myself each time that I fall.

I am awake from a deep slumber.
Happily ever what?
Hmm.
I wonder.

Disney movies.
I watched so many as a child.
Did I want to be a prince? Or a princess?
Looking back, that was wild.

Because Cinderella finally got her moment.
She overcame, achieved her greatness.
She won. She owned it.

When love led Jasmine to go against the norms
of societal classes to endure scrutiny after upsetting
regal masses,

When Ariel got a taste of a better aspect of life,
no longer submerged in her close-minded world,

Do you know the power that these messages have to a
little girl?

When true love and hard work led Tiana to victory
in her New Orleans dreams,

When Belle loved a beast,

When the world saw that the story of Pocahontas'
people
goes deeper than a feast...

******

Sometimes we get caught up in fairytale fantasies, like
when dissociative moments lead to a split. When you
snap back into your life, you realize how "that one"
wasn't "it." Every scholar knows the significance in the
hero's journey: to return to what once was, but in an
evolved state. We come back after life has beaten us
down and then offered us a clean slate.

Worry Wart

I'm not like other girls, but I can try to be.

It's exhausting,

Sitting by a trashcan fire next to a boy that I do not know, fake laughing as pubescent beer burps remind me of pickerel frog croaks.

Smokie

Great Grandma's hot comb press was no match for little wild Jess.

Country girl, better not make her wear a dress.

Racing barefoot on the pavement

Leaving trails of dust and gravel and chunks of grass

Knocking all the boys and girls down on their asses

Because she was still a superstar, back then.

A Shortened List of Baptist Church Songs

That bring forth memories of my childhood experiences that are hopefully not so common among other but also were not very pleasant times for me:

Precious Lord, Take My Hand

What a Friend We Have in Jesus

I Surrender All

Wade in the Water

Nothing But The Blood of Jesus

Amazing Grace

Down by the Riverside

Lift Every Voice and Sing

Swim

Immersion leads to
an unpleasant sting if I
stop kicking my legs.

ID

She gave herself permission to represent a bravery that she once felt unworthy of embodying. Solitary moments, sorting through layers of attached concepts and false notions of self, she discarded her own masks and met freedom.

Lost Diary Pages

Looking forward without succumbing to looking back,
yet
peripheral perspectives
May do me some good
No good are those kinda ties
That etch new regrets.

I have always had a conscience about my wrongdoings,
But there is this temporary bliss experienced when
living in denial.

There was something about reading "The Hatchet" as
a child.
Something about watching "Alice in Wonderland"
quite a few times.

There's something about a peculiar mind blessed to find
peace in pencil and paper
in all those hundreds of lost diary pages
years ago.

Patience

I'm not there yet,
and that's okay.
Beginners pace,
Residue in my hue.

Always looking within.

Cultivate.

Reiterate.

Self-awareness.

Patches Poem

Perspectives begin to shift leading to

Evolved ways of thinking, finally your

Resilience is making an impact, you are

Forming new norms as none of us have

Ever been perfect. These

Children must know

That we aren't superheroes, but humans who

Inevitably make mistakes,

Oftentimes living in our own denial creating

Negligent spaces leaving imprints and traces.

SURVIVAL MODE

CHIN UP CHEST OUT

DON'T COMPLAIN DON'T POUT.

SALUTE UP ABOUT-FACE

YOU CANNOT MAKE IT IN THIS RACE.

CHEST OUT, SHAMED AGAIN

I CANNOT DISSOCIATE AGAIN.

CHIN UP DON'T FRET

THESE ARE THE YEARS YOU'LL NEVER

GET

BACK. PRAY IT AWAY

THEY CAN'T HELP YOU.

NO NEED TO SAY

WHAT YOU WANT OR FEEL OR THINK

EMOTIONS ARE WEAK

CHIN UP CHEST OUT

CHILE, WHO ASKED YOU TO SPEAK?

MAKE MONEY CRY LATER

HANDS UP FIGHT BACK.

IT'S A DOG EAT DOG WORLD

ONLY WEIRD SINGLE WOMEN

LIKE CATS.

Whisper

Sometimes acceptance is acknowledging that there are conversations, the ones you really needed to have, that will never take place.

"Speak your mind, and don't feel guilty for it. You do know where shame and fear of being our true selves will lead us? Uh oh, I think I'm angry."

Sissy and I crack jokes that could land us in somebody's psych ward, but at least we can joke about trauma rather than use it as an excuse to do more dumb shit.

The mind is a terrible thing to waste, they say, but it is also a dangerous place to become lost in. My mind often longs to explode through my mouth, but rather than regurgitating all that is compacted within it, I'd like for it to come out sensibly.

******

"Get away from me. Something's wrong with you. I don't know what it is, but something's wrong."

Well, you're right about that. You've lost your mind, Mama. But you're happy and I love the look of happy on you.

Was your mind always as busy as mine is now? All this time? You must feel free now. It's time that I let go now, too.

CAT LADY POEM

You know how…

Your mind can scream so loudly

and you wanna shut down

You and you wanna shout out
"F this!"

But you told others to hold on
and you seemingly have become so strong

then you

Remember that you're human,
and a badass human at that

And how you've chosen to overcome things
And you've lived more lives
Than the cat they compare life stages to

Ambiguous hues in the label of a cat lady that
They used to try and scare you?

You know?

Breadcrumbs II

When I said that I don't have time to sit still, I should have said, "I can't sit still." That's the honesty that I like to uphold because if I'm going to do this right, I don't have time to sugar coat or make light of some real intense shit. I don't have time to sit still, sitting still causes me to overthink, why overthink when I can add a credential or three, or another degree to validate me.

But some doors aren't locked and there is no special key to get through. You open it and walk through, just as you.

Something that I can't shake is my innate state of perplexity, thinking about thinking about what I'm worried about, like my mind is always searching for something to fret about.

On the skin of my left shoulder there sits a beauty mole or a scar from pencil lead but the sentiment is still the same. I've got Mama's worrying nature, always preoccupied by what the world around me thinks of me.

TYPEWRITER

As of lately, I've grown fond of the look of cobblestone
and the idea of seclusion in a cute little cottage
surrounded by nature,
but I still have this damn phobia of bees, wasps, and
hornets.
Besides, I suppose I need a healthy social life.

Neuro Spiral

To say that there still aren't elements of fear after unpacking several layers of my own neurodivergence would be a lie. Plus I always over share, so of course there is a little fear there. Plus worry. If I wonder too long, it's as if a stairway opens up that first feels like elevation and discovery. Soon enough, there'll be a creak underneath my feet and I'll realize that the stairs are wooden planks erect from the starboard side of the ship that is my brain. Powerful, this thing, but it's still so very fragile.

WILT

Could I be as feral as a cat stuck in a tree?
Stuck studying those seeking reciprocity.

Could I be broken, an anarchist who dare not be
tamed?
I did say that the label "misfit" doesn't make me
ashamed.

And that one poem that I wrote about being a cat lady,
It does scream a lot, but there is this hazy

Sentiment leaving a film of felt on my tongue,
I can't clean up this jargon, soot sits on my lungs,

Spitting out unacceptable vernacular
Longing only to be and feel spectacular

Until I reach that place that is destined for me
And I walk into a room and demand my seat

I am not so uncultivated, ideas not too far-fetched,
Yes famished am I with my hand outstretched.

Double Dutch

My people, they drop like flies,
Pain and secrets disappear with their demise.

Some truths are hard to swallow,
Shot glass empty?
Pour her more.

My people, they deplete themselves
Playing double dutch to measure up
to cultural and societal expectations.
Tell me:
How attainable is it to meet both?

***She may as well put a lighter to that drink,
strong as gasoline and as potent as her delusions.***

I was never coordinated enough to
play double dutch, plus
all those girly girls were bullies anyway.

Instead, I'd sneak and watch rap music videos after
dark with Sleeping Beauty,
rebellion made us feel so alive.

Damn, I still wish that Sleeping Beauty would have
made it past 35.

Puzzle Pieces

My grandma can put together jigsaw puzzles with
thousands of pieces. I can tell that her mind is powerful.
They're all over, these beautiful puzzles: 3D puzzles,
transparent puzzles, landscape puzzles, family photo
puzzles, intricate models of famous and multicultural
and architectural puzzles. I could never sit still long
enough to piece together a puzzle more than 25 pieces;
too big a task that I'd surely leave incomplete. When I
was 17, I lost this journal that had a list of all the boys
and girls I "had crushes on." It disappeared, and I
never knew who found it.

Her Hero, She Is

Sit me in a room with the greats,

I am confident and capable of bringing my own plate -
my own table if need be.

Place me among the esteemed,

for now I see and acknowledge where I've been.

Sit me among those who weathered storms and had to
fight their own fight to overcome,
those who speak from learned lessons of life, not just
from their credentials.

Eleven

I don't think that old white lady knows that I know she didn't mean to run Max over. It's just that I'll never forget that day or his final, meek "wuff" before life left his brown eyes.

Buster's name wasn't that unique, but the way he took an eerie lean days before he left me sure was.

I don't know if Mama made herself forget about the old white man next door who likes to hug my neck each time she sends me to use his phone. It hurt, the thing he did real quick with his finger that last time.

Am I the only one who didn't forget about the dalmatian pup who died down in the basement? As summer came, the smell of his remains reminded us kids of our failures. I wonder what person finally stumbled upon that trash can ducked in the backyard.

Smiling Faces

Dear Little Jess,
You'll one day make friends who accept you as
you are and want the best for you. You won't have
to do anything extreme or go against who you are
in order to keep them. I promise.

******

Trust meets faith meets
Commitment meets stuck meets
Lingering hypocrisy meets
New friendships I can trust meets
Freedom meets destiny meets
Faces that smile genuinely meets
Stay for a while meets
I am not alone in my independence.

Worth Living For

Adverse Childhood Experiences Questionnaire for Adults

The night that I completed the ACEs Study Questionnaire, I felt excited. I used a 10-point scale format and ended up with a resulting score of 6. Heart pounding like the rhythm of an HBCU step show, yet I raced to tell no one.

What's worth living for is having a solid sense of self, even if it takes years to solidify who you are. Overcoming is what's worth living for. I am a success story, no longer needing to fill voids or dig into the pockets of my past to blame another human being or give anyone the power to tell my story.

There is no combusting here.
We learn from our mistakes here.
We speak truth with a little less vulgarity,
Clarity gained as liquid stained lies drip down the faces
of our enemies,
Here.

What a blessing it is to reflect on the past and not be engulfed by strong emotions that lead to actions that lead to regret and a sense of self-loathing. I own my past and all aspects of experiences that make me who I am today. I guess that makes me an adult, finally.

Until I reach that place that is destined for me
And I walk into a room and demand my seat

I am not so uncultivated, ideas not too far-
fetched,
Yes famished am I with my hand
outstretched.

About the Author

Written by poet and nonfiction author Jessica Fuller, "Lost Diary Pages" a collection of poetry and prose selections that tell a series of stories that scream "I am irrepressible." Jessica Fuller is a North Carolina native and a mother of three. She finds meaning in being a special education teacher and since age 11 has known that teaching and writing were included in her life's purpose.

Similar to her 2023 publication, "A Different Kind of Rising," Jessica leaves nonlinear reflections in a breadcrumb-like manner to connect her works.

Her use of fairytale character connotations makes this collection epiphany-like while disarranged pages of youth and adult "diary entries" bring forth compassion for the woven and interconnected nature of life trials amidst societal and intrinsic expectations.

Jessica uses references to movies like Alice in Wonderland and Fly Away Home while paying homage to the works and voices of Maya Angelou, Alice Walker, Audre Lorde, and Evie Shockley.

Jessica Fuller is the source behind the blog Jusjess Poetry, found at https://jusjesspoetry.org. Since launching her blog in 2022, she proudly disclaims, "I am writing my way into my destiny."

www.ingramcontent.com/pod-product-compliance
Lightning Source LLC
Chambersburg PA
CBHW071342130626
46556CB00005B/1986